Contents

HARDNESS OF HEART

Enemy of Faith

by **Andrew Wommack**

Hardness of Heart

Original editorial work by
John Calhoun Copywriting

Printed in the United States of America

Revised edition 2000
Editorial work by Bonnie Prestel

Acknowledgments

I wish to express my appreciation to:

<u>Kay Martin</u> —
for the hours transcribing the tapes.

<u>Cindi Deville</u> —
for the layout, proofreading, and editorial work.

<u>Mike Martin</u> —
for handling all the details.

Introduction

It is my prayer the Lord will give you ears to hear the message of this book, so that you can experience the fullness of God's blessing and, in return, be the blessing to others the Lord intends you to be.

Many believers have come to share the conviction that God is still doing miracles today, just as He did in Bible times. They rejoice at testimonies of others who experience these miracles yet, in most cases, they do not experience all the blessings of the Lord themselves.

Add to this the fact that testimonies pour in from foreign lands of people hearing the gospel for the first time, and their blind eyes open or their crippled limbs are made whole, and our frustration rises. Why do these people with no knowledge of faith, no time in prayer or Bible study receive and we don't? How can this be?

The Lord gave me the answer to this question, and many others, through this teaching on hardness of heart. I believe these truths will become the basis for many things God wants to do in your life.

Andrew Wommack

Part 1:
The Crisis

Hardness of heart has stricken all Christians in some area of their lives. This is what keeps us from hearing the voice of the Lord and being led by Him in our everyday lives.

1

The Feeding
of the 5,000

In Mark 6:35-44, Jesus fed 5,000 men—probably 15,000 people in all—with five loaves and two fish; and He had more left over than He started with! That was a pretty notable miracle, but something even more amazing was about to happen.

In verses 45-48, it says, *"And straightway he constrained his disciples to get into the ship, and go to the other side before unto Bethsaida, while he sent away the people. And when he had sent them away, he departed into a mountain to pray. And when even was come, the ship was in the midst of the sea, and he alone on the land. And he saw them toiling and rowing; for the wind was contrary unto them: and about the fourth watch of the night he cometh unto them, walking upon the sea, and would have passed by them."*

Sore Amazed

As I was reading this, I wondered what it would be like to be one of these disciples, with a storm about to kill me. Here comes Jesus, walking on the water—that's amazing in itself—but it says He would have passed by them. You'd think Jesus would run out there yelling, "Here I am to help you!" I was amazed, to say the least.

Exactly the same thing happened to the disciples. Verse 49 says, *"But when they saw him walking upon the sea, they supposed it had been a spirit, and cried out:"* In other words, they couldn't believe it was Jesus. They thought they were seeing a vision. Verses 50-51 say, *"For they all saw him and were troubled. And immediately he talked with them, and saith unto them, Be of good cheer: it is I; be not afraid. And he went up unto them into the ship; and the wind ceased: and they were sore amazed in themselves beyond measure, and wondered."*

Sore amazed! That's putting it mildly. I was awe-struck when I thought of preparing to die, seeing Jesus walking on the water that was about to kill me, then watching him act as if He was going to pass right by.

Apply this to your situation. For example, maybe you are struggling with a desperate financial problem. Maybe your marriage is falling apart. Maybe the doctor told you you're going to die of cancer. Here comes Jesus saying, "Oh, a million dollars...saving a marriage...healing a sickness...that's nothing," and then He walks right on by you. You would be "sore amazed," right?

Then I read verse 52, which says, *"For they considered not the miracle of the loaves: for their heart was hardened."* "For, " of course, is a conjunction, and it links verse 52 to verse 51. It is inferring that they shouldn't have been sore amazed—it should not have been surprising to see Jesus walk on the water.

Hardness of Heart

Why were they amazed? It says it was because of their *hardness of heart*.

Something began to dawn on me. I had always thought hardness of heart applied to someone who was rebellious toward God, who hated God. For example, I got saved when I was eight years old, and since then my desire has always been to seek God with my whole heart. I never thought of myself as hard-hearted. Yet the Lord was saying, in effect, "If you'd be surprised to see Jesus walking on the water or any other supernatural manifestation of God, you're hard-hearted."

I had to start reconsidering what hardness of heart was.

Not Just Rebellion

Hardness of heart is not just rebellion towards God. Hardness of heart, in its simplest sense, is *relating more easily to the natural realm than to the supernatural.*

If that's true, it means that every one of us is hard-hearted toward God to some extent—we're more moved by what we see than we're supposed to be. We should reach a place where we're more moved by what *God* says than we are by anything else.

For example, in reading this, some of you will be totally set free, and others will say, "That's the deadest thing I've ever read; I didn't get a thing out of it." It's not me, the writer, who is the variable. For instance, when I teach, all the people in the audience hear the same message. Some receive it and their lives are changed. Others seem to get nothing out of it. The difference isn't me—or the message. The difference is the condition of their hearts.

Morality is No Help

You can be hardened toward God and yet be a good, moral person. I've never said a cussword in my entire life. I've never taken a drink of liquor. I've never smoked a cigarette. I've never done a lot of things that you may have done, but I had a very hard heart towards God, and I still do in some areas. Hardness of heart is not only caused by rebellion or sin.

One of the characteristics of a hardened heart is that it will make you amazed at the power of God. You'll relate more easily to the natural than to the supernatural.

When Jesus fed those 5,000 people, I believe He was blessed, but I don't believe He cried, "Wow! Look at that! It worked! Praise God!" Jesus was not shocked; I believe He totally expected it. He would have been amazed if it hadn't worked. When many of us pray and don't see the desired result, we say, "Well, that's kind of what I expected." Most of us would be amazed to see something miraculous happen.

I Crossed My Own Prayers

I once prayed for a young boy in Omaha, Nebraska, whose eyes were crossed. They were so bad he couldn't even see where I was standing. I commanded his eyes to straighten out, and they were immediately straight as an arrow. You know what I did? I said, "I can't believe it." Do you know what they did? They went right back to where they were before. As far as I know, they're still crossed.

That's hardness of heart—and it stopped my faith.

Let's continue in Mark, chapter eight, looking at some other characteristics of a hard heart. Mark 8:1-3 says, *"In those days the multitude being very great, and having nothing to eat, Jesus called his disciples unto him, and saith unto them, I have compassion on the multitude, because they have now been with me three days, and have nothing to eat: And if I send them away fasting to their own houses, they will faint by the way: for divers of them came from far."*

In the previous feeding of the 5,000 recorded in John 6:5, we see where Jesus turned to Philip when He saw the multitude, and said, *"Whence shall we buy bread, that these may eat?"*

Do you suppose Jesus was wringing his hands, saying, "Oh, disciples, what are we going to do? How are we possibly going to feed all these people?" No, He knew what He was going to do. In fact, verse six says, *"And this he said to prove him: for he himself knew what he would do.* " Jesus wasn't asking the question of Philip to gain information, but rather to give the disciples an opportunity to act on it in faith.

The Disciples Fail

But they failed. Philip pulled out his wallet and said, *"Two hundred pennyworth of bread is not sufficient for them. . ."* (verse 7).

Now, a few days later, the exact same situation occurred. This time there were seven loaves and 4,000 men—more food to work with and fewer people to feed. Jesus had already shown them what He could do, but He was trying to get his disciples involved in this miracle.

This time, Philip could have said, "Jesus, I know what to do. We'll take these loaves and fishes and feed this entire multitude, just like before." Do you know what the disciples did? Mark 8:4 says, *"And his disciples answered him, From whence can a man satisfy these men with bread here in the wilderness?"* They failed again.

Why didn't they remember? It was only a few days later, but they had totally forgotten what God had done; they had forgotten the miracle. We think, *Boy, how could they be so dumb? Didn't they remember what had happened?*

How many of you have ever had a miracle of God happen in your life and thought, *I'll never, never doubt God again,* then the next day, something bad happens, and it throws you totally into reverse? You totally forgot about what God did the previous day. That's hardness of heart.

Beware the Leaven

Let's continue in Mark, chapter eight. After feeding the 4,000 people, Jesus said in verses 15-17, *"And he charged them, saying, Take heed, beware [of] the leaven of the Pharisees, and of the leaven of Herod. And they reasoned among themselves, saying, [It is] because we have no bread. And when Jesus knew it, he saith unto them, Why reason ye, because ye have not bread? perceive ye not yet, neither understand? have ye your heart yet hardened?"*

Again, Jesus is talking about hardness of heart—exactly what He rebuked the disciples for in chapter six. This time, He gives a little more explanation of what it is. It's *not perceiving or understanding*. It doesn't mean that you don't know the truth; it simply means that you don't perceive that truth in a way that will change you.

He continues in verses 18-21: *"Having eyes, see ye not? and having ears, hear ye not? and do ye not remember? When I brake the five loaves among five thousand, how many baskets full of fragments took ye up? They say unto him, Twelve. And when the seven among four thousand, how many baskets full of fragments took ye up? And they said, Seven. And He said unto them, How is it that ye do not understand?"*

Just the Facts Won't Do

The disciples had knowledge. They remembered the facts, but those facts didn't influence their behavior. They didn't change their circumstances. That knowledge was non-productive, because they didn't have the spiritual perception and the wisdom to use it. Again, that's hardness of heart.

The Bible has much to say about this. We'll cover it in more depth in the next chapter.

2

Other
Examples

When the Israelites came out of Egypt, they saw great, miraculous things. They crossed the Red Sea, they saw nine plagues on Egypt, they had a pillar of fire cover them by night, and a cloud by day. Yet just two or three days later, they were asking, "Can God provide a table in the wilderness? Can God feed all of this multitude?"

You may ask, "How could they do that? How could they be so dense?" Hebrews, chapter three, says the reason the children of Israel were like that was the *hardness of their hearts*.

Pharaoh—The Supreme Example

Pharaoh is the supreme example of hard-heartedness. Look at him in Exodus, chapter eight and beyond. The

Bible mentions Pharaoh's heart being hardened at least 18 times. When God hardens your heart, you're in trouble. (Under the new covenant, God does not harden our hearts.)

Pharaoh saw all these miracles. He saw the plagues on Egypt, and right after each plague, he'd harden his heart and persist in his ways. For example, when the plague of the frogs came, frogs were everywhere—frogs were in their shoes, in their food, in their clothes. They literally covered the land. Finally, Pharaoh called Moses and said, "Moses, I've sinned this time. It's God." He had sinned before that, but now he finally realized it. He came to his senses, humbled himself and admitted that it was God who was doing all this.

He implored Moses, "Remove this plague from me." And Moses said, "Glory over me. Tell me when I should remove this plague."

Now watch what hardness of heart can do. Understand, Pharaoh was *plagued*—humbled, destroyed and brought to his knees. He could have asked for the frogs to leave instantly. But when he was asked, he said, "Tomorrow." Now that's being hard-hearted. That's being void of judgment. That's being dense, but that's exactly what hardness of heart does.

Of course, he hardened himself more and more, until he finally *was* destroyed in the Red Sea.

What About You?

How does this apply to you? Hardness of heart does not mean that you don't know what is true in your head, but it means that knowledge is not productive.

For example, if I were to ask, "Quote me a healing scripture," you could probably rattle off Isaiah 53:5, Matthew 8:17, 1 Peter 2:24, 3 John 2, and so forth. Yet a lot of you are sick. Is God's Word not producing? Some of you may say, "Well, I just don't know enough; I need to learn more." If that's true, then no one who has just been born again could ever see a miracle. Many of us saw *more* miracles happen then than we do now, and we knew less.

Smith Wigglesworth

Many of the great men of faith—Smith Wigglesworth, John Lake, William Branham—knew less of the Word of God than you and I know, but they saw more happen.

Not a Leg to Stand On

Smith Wigglesworth, for example, once spent the night with a man who had both legs amputated. As they talked about healing, Smith suddenly said to him, "Go and buy a pair of new shoes in the morning." Then Smith went to bed. As the man thought about this, the Lord spoke to him and told him to do exactly as Smith had said.

First thing in the morning, he went down to the shoe store and asked the clerk for a pair of shoes. The clerk said, "What size?" When the clerk saw that he wanted them for himself, he said, "Sir, I can't help you." So the man said, "Give me a pair of eight regular in black." The clerk gave him the shoes, the man paid for them, and he took them out of the box. He put one shoe on one nub and a leg and a foot instantly grew into the shoe! He put the other shoe on the other nub, and a leg and a foot instantly grew into that shoe.

Obviously, this was a great miracle, but that man didn't know as much about faith as most of us today.

If what we know is so much greater, why don't we see those kind of miracles? Hardness of heart.

T. L. Osborne

T.L. Osborne, the evangelist, has probably seen as many people healed as any other person who ever lived, including Jesus, because he's ministered to more people through mass meetings. In his overseas meetings, he seldom finishes his message, as the blind start seeing, the lame start walking, and the deaf start hearing. Sometimes 100,000 people will be healed in one night. There is so much commotion, he has to stop the message and invite people to get born again.

Yet when that same man ministers in the United States, very little happens. When he ministered on Robert Tilton's satellite network, for example, a friend of mine who had his legs blown off in Vietnam was at the service. He said that of over 2,000 people there, the most healed on any night were 12—and he wasn't one of them.

We know more, but we're seeing less in many cases. Some people have never heard the gospel before, but if they hear somebody just *mention* that Jesus heals, they'll get out of their wheelchairs. They'll throw their crutches down. They'll be healed instantly.

Why? Because the word of God *penetrates* their hearts. For most of us, it doesn't.

Proverbs, 4:20-22 says, *"My son, attend to my words; incline thine ear unto my sayings. Let them not depart from thine eyes; keep them in the midst of thine heart. For they are life unto those that find them, and health to all their flesh."*

I was meditating on this one day and asked, "God, what does 'incline thine ear' mean?" God told me that He is not talking about the position you hold your head in! What He's talking about is how you pay attention.

An Earful in Vietnam

Let me give you a really vivid example: When I was in Vietnam, I was on a fire support base. There were always bombs going off, rockets being fired, mortars blasting away. Often, we'd take 10 or 15 direct hits a day, one or two of them right on top of my bunker. The bunker withstood it, but it would knock everything off the shelf and create a cloud of dust. Finally, I got used to it. *I learned to tune it out.*

One day, I pulled guard duty in a bunker named Bunker Number One. It was about a hundred yards farther down the hill than the others, so it was more exposed to enemy fire. There were four of us on duty. I had the first watch. Two of the guys went below to sleep, and the other fellow, a Puerto Rican, stayed on top with me. He was a draftee, and the only English he spoke was "forty days"— no matter what you asked him, he answered, "forty days." He was slightly crazy. He took the second watch and I went to sleep right next to him, on top of the bunker.

About five o'clock in the morning, I woke up and he wasn't there. I looked below and the other two guys weren't there either. We were supposed to stay on guard duty until six o'clock, so I stayed and then went back up the hill. Suddenly, this huge procession of officers, soldiers and the chaplain ran up to me and asked, "Are you all right?" I answered, "Sure." I didn't know what they were talking about.

It turned out that this Puerto Rican fellow had gone completely berserk in the night and had shot off everything we had. He shot something like 500 or 600 M-16 rounds, threw over 100 hand grenades, shot 100 or more grenade launchers, and detonated every Claymore mine in our position (these things could bounce you right off the ground and even deafen you). He was shooting up the hill, down the hill—everywhere. The guys below got scared and ran off.

The others up the hill were going to blow him away, but they knew I was there, so they held off. Finally, he ran out of ammunition, walked up the hill, and they grabbed him.

I slept right through the whole thing!

On the other hand, if anybody walked into my bunker when I was asleep, the door, just creaking on its hinge, would instantly awaken me.

Why? It's because *I had inclined my ear* to hear the things that were threatening. The explosions were normal, but anything abnormal, like footsteps, was threatening. The same thing has probably happened to you.

You may live on a busy street or in the flight path of an airport. Yet you can get used to those noises and tune them out, but the sound of your baby crying will instantly awaken you.

The Choice is Yours

The same thing happens in the supernatural. You can be sensitive to what you want to. You can be hardened to what you want to.

Many people complain to me that they can't remember scripture, no matter how hard they try. They ask me how I do it (I've been accused of having a photographic memory, but that's not the case). Yet these same people can tell me who won the World Series or the Super Bowl, and all the relevant statistics. I can't remember any of those things. I even watch the Super Bowl sometimes and can't remember who won!

There is nothing wrong with their memories or mine. It's just that a hardened heart dulls your memory (Mk. 8:18). Your memory is linked to your heart. What your heart is sensitive to, you'll remember; what your heart is hardened to, you'll forget.

Back to Egypt

Let's continue with Pharaoh. After all of those plagues, after the frogs, after his firstborn was killed, after all this misery, he finally let the children of Israel go. Even his own officer said, "Let them go or Egypt is destroyed" (Ex. 10:7). Pharaoh had been defeated and he acknowledged it. He told Moses, "If you ever see my face again, I'll kill you" (Ex. 10:28).

Then, the Bible says that God hardened Pharaoh's heart. Immediately, he lost all of his perception, all of his wisdom, all of his thinking capacity, and went after the children of Israel. It would be impossible for anybody to be that irrational without help!

The children of Israel were camped, with the Red Sea on one side and the mountains on the other; they were in the valley in between. Pharaoh and his armies came upon them and saw them trapped there. Contrary to Hollywood's depiction of this, they did not cross in daylight. They crossed at night.

The Pillar of Fire

The Bible says a pillar of fire went in front of the children of Israel (Ex. 13:21-22). When they were at the Red Sea, it came down and settled in the valley between them and the Egyptians (Ex. 14:19). Now, if you're hardhearted enough to chase the Israelites after they had just beaten the most powerful nation on earth, it seems you'd wise up when the supernatural fire of God appeared. But the Bible says that the Egyptians stayed over 12 hours looking at that fire!

Moreover, the pillar gave light to the Israelites, and darkness to the Egyptians (Ex. 14:20). It's one thing to have a fire standing in your way, but another to see that fire producing darkness for you and light for your enemies! Pharaoh just sat there until the fire dissipated while the Israelites crossed the Red Sea. Then he started after them.

The Bible then says that the Lord took their chariot wheels off, so that they drove them heavily. I would imagine so—without any wheels! Finally, some of those really sharp Egyptians said, "The Lord is fighting for the Israelites." Boy, I think I could have figured that out before, don't you? *That's* hardness of heart.

By then, of course, it was too late—the sea collapsed and destroyed the Egyptians completely.

The point is that when your heart is hardened, you don't reason correctly. How many times have you done something that was really dumb and later told God, "Lord, how could I have been so dumb?" You really knew back then what you should have done, yet it didn't occur to you in the midst of your problem. It shows that you had a hardened heart towards the things of God. Hardness of heart produces spiritual retardation. In Job 39:13-17, the Lord speaks to Job about the ostrich. He says the ostrich buries her eggs in the sand and then forgets that they may be stepped on or eaten by wild beasts. Verse 16 says it's because she is *hardened* against her young. Verse 17 further defines this hardening as being deprived of wisdom and understanding.

It's Reversible!

Up until now, all I've talked about is hardness of heart: the bad news.

But did you know it's reversible? You can become sensitive to God and hardened to the world. If you can analyze how hardness of heart starts, you can stop it and reverse it to the point that one word from God will nullify hundreds of words from the devil! Jesus says in John 10:4-5, *"...and the sheep follow him: for they know his voice. And a stranger will they not follow, but will flee from him: for they know not the voice of strangers."* It says believers can hear the voice of God, and ignore the voice of the devil.

In the next section, we will talk about how hardness of heart originates. That's the first step in learning to overcome it.

Part 2: The Cause

It doesn't matter what we know, it's what we think on that controls whether our hearts are hard or soft (Prov. 23:7).

3

Why Hardness of Heart Comes

In this section, we'll talk about how hardness of heart originates. We've already established that it's something that affects just about everybody, even those seeking God.

Harden Not Your Heart

Hebrews 3:7-12 says, *"Wherefore (as the Holy Ghost saith, Today if ye will hear his voice, Harden not your hearts, as in the provocation, in the day of temptation in the wilderness: When your fathers tempted me, proved me, and saw my works forty years. Wherefore I was grieved with that generation, and said, They do always err in their heart; and they have not known my ways. So I sware in my wrath, They shall not enter into my rest.) Take heed, breth-*

ren, lest there be in any of you an evil heart of unbelief, in departing from the living God."

What do we see here? First, this passage of scripture shows that you are the one who hardens your heart. As I said earlier, God doesn't harden your heart (God did harden Pharaoh's heart, but that was under a different covenant than we have).

Second, in verse 12, it talks about having an *evil heart of unbelief.* When your heart is hardened, the immediate result is unbelief. If your heart is not hardened, you will not have unbelief.

Then, in verse 13 it says, *"But exhort one another daily, while it is called Today; lest any of you be hardened through the deceitfulness of sin."* So it says that your heart can become hardened through the *deceitfulness of sin.*

What About Sin?

I won't devote a lot of space to sin, because we've all heard sin preached a lot, and no born-again person consciously wants to sin. I'll just say this: if you're living in sin, stop it, because it's going to harden your heart. You cannot live in sin and have a heart sensitive towards God.

Sin is not the only thing that will stop our faith. It is not even the main thing.

Take my life, for example. I was brought up in a denomination that preached, "Live a holy life, be good, and don't sin." I was born again when I was eight years old, the first time I was ever convicted by God of sin. As a result, I've never said a cussword, taken a drink, or smoked a cigarette in my whole life. I've followed God to the best of my ability.

When I was born again, I asked, "What is sin?" They told me, "Don't drink or cuss or dip or chew, or go with those who do"—that was about it. Well, I didn't do any of that. I wasn't sinning by their definition. I was living a holy life, yet I still wasn't seeing the power of God manifested. For example, I saw my father die when I was 12 years old, and a number of other people, too. I was with them when they died. I was praying for them to be healed, and they weren't.

I want to drive this point home, because some people think that if they live holy lives, everything will work. It's not your holiness that produces. If it were, I'd have a lot of you beat! We don't get anything from God through our holiness; none of us can be that holy. It's either God's grace or nothing.

It's not just sin that ensnares us; there are other things as well. For example, in Hebrews 12:1, it says, *"...let us lay aside every weight, and the sin which doth so easily beset [us]...."* You can be encumbered by *weights* and you will still lose the race. So there are a lot of other things that can affect us, but I'm only going to deal with one area, because I believe it is the key. If you deal with this area, everything else will fall into line.

What You See is What You Get

I'll make this point now and then substantiate it through much of this book—*whatever you focus your at-*

tention on is what will dominate you. Conversely, whatever you don't focus on cannot dominate you.

Let's look again at Mark, chapter six, where we started. Remember that the disciples were *"...sore amazed in themselves beyond measure and wondered"* (v. 51). Verse 52 gives you the explanation why. It says that they were hard-hearted, and the reason was that they *considered not the [miracle] of the loaves*. Notice the reason was not sin—they had not been in rebellion toward God. They did not say, "I don't believe in Jesus." They did not have a pornographic magazine on board. They were not drunk in the boat.

Their hearts were hardened because they *considered not* the miracle of the loaves. They neglected what God had done in their presence, and didn't give it priority.

On the other hand, if they had meditated *totally* on what Jesus did—feeding 5,000 people with five loaves and two fish—that would have ministered faith to them. They would have said, "Look who Jesus is, look at the power He has, look at the dominion He has! Nothing is impossible to Jesus. If He can feed 5,000 people He can surely walk on water!" They wouldn't have been surprised to see Jesus walking on water if they would have kept their minds stayed upon that miracle. They would have been praying, "God, send Jesus out here to save us."

What you don't consider—what you neglect—is what you're going to be hardened to.

Natural or Supernatural?

Why were the disciples so hardened?

Look at Mark 6:45: *"And straightway he constrained his disciples to get into the ship, and to go to the other side before unto Bethsaida, while he sent away the people."* The word "constrained" means that Jesus had to put a little pressure on his disciples to get into that ship. They apparently did not want to get in. Why? The Bible doesn't tell us exactly, but let's read between the lines for a moment.

These men were fishermen. Their lives depended, among other things, on being able to see what kind of weather was coming into the area. On the Sea of Galilee, violent storms come down out of the mountains in a short time, and if you don't see them, you can be drowned out there. Those men had their senses exercised for weather. I believe they could tell that there was a storm coming. I also believe that is why they didn't want to go, but because of their love and commitment to Jesus, they went ahead.

When they got out on the water, the storm hit and confirmed everything their senses were telling them. Immediately, they began to draw on every bit of knowledge they had to save their lives. Most of us think, *That's just natural.* Yes, that is natural, but in this case it was wrong because God had constrained them to go to the other side. If they had kept their minds stayed on Jesus instead of lapsing into the natural realm, they would have been expecting the miraculous.

This is the same instance quoted in Matthew, chapter 14, where Peter walked on the water. Jesus rebuked the disciples because of the hardness of their hearts: their doubt and unbelief. In effect, He said, "Look, guys, you should have been able to control this storm yourselves. Where's your faith?"

The Bell Tolls for Us

This is where the church is today. Certain segments of the church are living in rebellion and sin, but the vast majority isn't. Most of you love God, but if you're honest about it, you'd say you're not confident in your ability to overcome Satan in the area of sickness and disease. You don't have a confidence, you don't have a boldness, you don't know that you're a world-overcomer. If someone near you was dying right now, you might call me or your pastor or some other "man of faith" to pray for him, but if you were asked to pray for him, that's different. You aren't confident in your own ability. It's not because you've been living in rebellion and sin; it's because you've neglected the things of God.

We've not *considered* the things of God. This subject is so important we're going to devote an entire chapter to it.

4

What You Consider is What You Get

The word "consider" means, "to take into account, to ponder, to study, to examine, to deliberate upon" (NAHD). To sum it up: to meditate. As I said before, what you spend your time considering is what will dominate you. Nothing can happen to you unless you conceive it in your thought life; you can't sin unless you think sin!

In this chapter, we'll look at several examples, both in and outside of the Bible, that illustrate this truth.

First, look at James 1:14-15. It says, *"But every man is tempted, when he is drawn away of his own lust, and enticed. Then when lust hath conceived, it bringeth forth sin: and sin, when it is finished, bringeth forth death."*

Notice, it says you have to be drawn away by your own lust—nobody just breaks away from God. After that, lust has to conceive. That is exactly like a baby being conceived. Sin is the same: it has to be conceived. How is it conceived? It's through your lust, what you think upon. For example, if you went to a primitive country and started showing the people all of our fancy western gadgets, they might eventually become necessities to them; they might even get to the point that they'd kill for them! But before that point, when they didn't have them, they couldn't be tempted with them. That principle is present throughout the Bible, right from the beginning.

The Fall—Hearing was Involved

In Genesis, chapter three, we read the story of the fall. Notice in reading it that Satan was not able to come and just make Eve sin. He had to tempt her, and he did so by talking to her. In other words, she had to hear something. What you hear is going to affect you. Jesus said, *"Take heed what ye hear. . ."* (Mk. 4:24). In I Corinthians 15:33 Paul says, *"Be not deceived: evil communications corrupt good manners."*

Satan was talking to Eve about the tree of the knowledge of good and evil. Genesis 3:6 says, *"And when the woman saw that the tree was good for food, and that it was pleasant to the eyes, and a tree to be desired to make one wise, she took of the fruit thereof, and did eat, and gave also unto her husband with her; and he did eat."* It says, *"And when the woman saw. . . ."* The scripture implies that the woman did not focus her attention on this tree until Satan pointed it out. She never considered it, so she was never tempted by it.

We could not be tempted with disbelieving God if we did not consider something other than God's Word. The Bible says, *"So then faith cometh by hearing, and hearing by the word of God"* (Rom. 10:17). If all you do is meditate on the Word of God, then all you can do is believe God. It's that simple. If you've been tempted with doubt and unbelief, it is because you've been thinking about something other than the Word of God.

Abraham—Man of Little Unbelief

Let's look at the life of Abraham. In Hebrews, chapter 11, it says that Abraham was a great man of faith, but Abraham really didn't have as much faith as you and I have. Abraham actually had less than you and I have—less doubt and unbelief! Abraham was a great man because of what he did not consider, what he did not focus his attention on. Verse 15 says of Abraham and his family, *"And truly, if they had been mindful of that country from whence they came out, they might have had opportunity to have returned."* In other words, the chance to return to Ur of the Chaldees would have been linked directly to what they thought. Or, you could turn it around to say: if they weren't mindful of the country they left, they couldn't have been tempted to return.

What really made Abraham strong was not his great faith, but his discipline over his own thoughts. You and I could be great men and women of faith if we were not tempted to disbelieve God, or if we weren't so well trained in doubt and unbelief.

Romans 4:18-19 says of Abraham, *"Who against hope believed in hope, that he might become the father of many nations, according to that which was spoken, So shall they seed be. And being not weak in faith, he considered not his own body now dead, when he was about an hundred years old, nor yet the deadness of Sarah's womb...."* *"Considered not"*—this is the same language used in Mark, chapter 6, speaking of the disciples. Since Abraham didn't consider it, he could not be tempted with disbelieving God.

When the angel finally appeared to Abraham and told him that in the next year his wife would bear a child, it was not the first time he heard it. The key to his believing lay 26 years *before*, when God first gave him the promise. For all those 26 years, all Abraham thought was, *"According to the stars in the sky and the sand on the seashore, so shall my seed be."* So when the promise came, Abraham was well-disciplined—that's why he saw the miracle. Most of us are not like that. We are not well-disciplined.

Isaac—Son of Promise

Look at Abraham's son, Isaac. I used to ask myself: How could Abraham possibly offer up Isaac for a sacrifice? I once saw a movie, in which Abraham was called by God to offer his son. The movie shows Abraham ramming his fist into a wall and screaming, "Oh, no, God, not Isaac!" Then after agonizing and arguing with God all night, Abraham finally summons up all the courage within him and goes up to offer Isaac.

The Bible doesn't show us that picture. It never implies that Abraham dragged his feet, complained, or said a single negative thing. He simply rose up early in the morning, went to Mt. Moriah, about a three-day's journey away, and started up the mountain. Isaac, who was about 17, asked, "Father, here's the wood and here's the fire, but where's the offering?" Abraham did not answer, "Son, you're the offering." He said, "My son, God will provide himself a lamb for a burnt offering..." (Gen. 22:8). Notice that he didn't say, "God himself shall provide," but said, "God shall provide *himself ....*" (Mt. Moriah, by the way, is the location where God later built the temple. Some experts believe that the Holy of Holies stood on the exact spot where Abraham offered the sacrifice, so this event has tremendous significance.)

Hebrews 11:17-18 says, *"By faith Abraham, when he was tried, offered up Isaac: and he that had received the promises offered up his only begotten son, Of whom it was said, That in Isaac shall thy seed be called...."* Then, verse 19 gives us an insight into what Abraham was thinking: *"Accounting that God [was] able to raise [him] up, even from the dead; from whence also he received him in a figure."* Abraham did not think, *God, how could I stand to see the blood run out of Isaac and know that I am responsible?* Abraham didn't picture what it would be like without Isaac. *He didn't see him dead.* He wasn't tempted by all the things that accompany those thoughts.

A Better Covenant

In Matthew, chapter 11, and 2 Corinthians, chapter three, the Bible says that Abraham's covenant is inferior to what you and I have. We have much more of the power and grace of God than Abraham did, yet he did something that most of us wouldn't even consider doing. Why? Because Abraham did not *consider* (there is that word again) his son dead. He considered that God would raise him from the dead if necessary, so Abraham wasn't even tempted not to offer him.

Abraham was a great man of God because of what he considered—or *didn't* consider. We can be the same way.

New York, New York, What a Sinful City

Let me illustrate this point in my own life. As I said earlier, the Lord preserved me from much of the sin that others, maybe you, got into. Because of that, I was hardened toward sin. I just grew up that way.

For example, when I was 18 years old, my mother took me on a trip across Europe. Before our tour group left, we spent the night in New York City. I had *never* in my life, seen the kind of sin I saw on Broadway and 45th Street. I was literally amazed. I was walking down the street one night witnessing to gang members (I didn't know any better back then), when suddenly, a pimp came up to me and tried to sell me one of his girls. I didn't even know what he was talking about!

When I got back to the motel room, I told the other guys in the group, "You'll never believe what this guy was telling me. It didn't make any sense at all." They all began to make fun of me, saying, "You dummy! Don't you know what he was trying to do?" I didn't, so I wasn't the least bit tempted; it would have been impossible for me to respond to it. I didn't know enough to respond.

What You Don't Know Can't Hurt You

I once was counseling a man in Salt Lake City over the phone. He began confessing all of his sexual sins, and said, "Well, you know how it is. You were single once." But I had to be honest and tell him, "Listen, fella, I was married, had two children, and pastored three churches before I learned about perversion; I learned it through counseling. I didn't know anybody had those thoughts."

I didn't know that sexual perversion was an option; therefore, I didn't have to fight a battle to overcome that temptation. That's a blessing.

In Romans 16:19, Paul says, *"...I would have you wise unto that which is good, and simple concerning evil."* It seems that we've turned that around. We're wise about that which is evil (we know every negative thing), and simple about that which is good.

Just What the Doctor Ordered?

For example, when the doctor says, "You're going to die of cancer," most of us automatically respond, "Well, show me why. Give me a detailed medical picture." We talk to someone whose uncle died of cancer, we read about it in a magazine. We get all the details so we can consider it, think about it, and dwell upon it, then we wonder why *"by His stripes ye were healed"* doesn't work for us. We haven't given as much time to meditating on *"by His stripes"* as we have on cancer. We've had it instilled into us from childhood that you can't ignore these things—*the doctor says so.*

It seems that medical people are the hardest people of all to see healed. That's because they were only told one side in medical school. For example, they were told that when you see a tumor that appears a certain way, the next step is death. They don't counter it with, "This is the way the *natural* says it is, but God can intervene and change all that." They weren't taught that. Their minds are so geared to the natural world that even now, after they're born again, they have a hard time receiving a miracle because they relate more easily to the natural than to the Word of God.

Smith Wigglesworth: A Separated Life

What we're taught, what the world instills in us, has a major effect on our faith, or lack of it. The reason it gets into us is because we don't separate ourselves from it.

Do you know what made Smith Wigglesworth and others like him such miracle workers? A *separated* life. Now people have misinterpreted that. They say it was their holiness—that if you have any sin in your life, God won't use you, and if you're totally pure, He will. That's foolish, because you can never be good enough. It was not their holiness that earned them anything from God. But their separation sensitized them to what they *already* had from God. They focused all of their attention on it. They didn't allow temptation to enter.

One of the criticisms spoken against Smith Wigglesworth was that he was cold, insensitive, unfeeling, and unyielding (that's the definition of hardened). He was cold, insensitive, unfeeling, and unyielding to anything but God! He did not pity people with disease and sickness. That sounds extreme, but never in over 40 years of ministry did he lay his hands on a person who wasn't healed.

A Tumor Vanishes

A woman in one of Smith's meetings had a huge tumor. In his meetings, Smith would often say, "The first person to stand up will be healed of whatever problem he has." He said that and this lady, with two other ladies holding her up, stood up. She was in terrible pain and her legs were so thin she could not stand by herself. They took her up on the platform and Smith said, "Let her go." The two ladies with her answered, "She can't stand if we let her go—she'll fall." So he said again, "Let her go."

They let her go, and she fell over with a thud. You could imagine what the crowd thought. Smith said, "Pick her up." So they picked her up, and again he said, "Let her go." They said, "We can't let her go, she'll fall," so he raised his voice and said, "Let her go!" They let her go, and she fell again, crying out in pain. So they picked her up, and for the third time he said, "Let her go." They answered, "We will not let her go—that's cruel," so he raised his voice again and said, "Let her go!" They answered, "No!"

Just then, a man stood up in the audience and yelled, "You callous brute—leave her alone!" Smith yelled back at him, "You mind your own business. I know mine." He yelled again and said, "Let her go!" They let her go, and that tumor just fell off on the floor. She walked right out of there healed.

Do you know why it worked for him? Because whenever he saw something contrary to what God had told him, he hardened himself to it. He was hardened to his senses, even his good, natural senses, so that he was not moved by anything except what God had told him. That's why it worked.

My Own Attempt

Now consider what I did once. I was ministering to a man in Sioux City, Iowa, who was in a wheelchair. I had faith—this was *after* I'd seen two people raised from the dead. I knew God had told me to minister to him. I went up to him, prayed, grabbed him by the hands and lifted him out of that chair. He fell right to the floor. I picked him up, and immediately thought, *Oh God, look what I've done. I've caused him pain. I've embarrassed him.* So I began to consider him and his situation. I began to consider what people thought. I began to consider everything but what God had told me to do. Eventually, I ended up putting him back in the wheelchair, and he stayed there. I didn't give him what he needed. I didn't do what Wigglesworth did.

Later, I went back to the motel room thinking, *God, what's wrong?* It was years before I learned that the same thing had happened to Smith Wigglesworth, but Smith just kept at it, while I was moved away from my faith by the hardness of my heart. I was still more sensitive to the natural realm than to the supernatural. It was a lifestyle that I'd been developing all my life; the unbelief started years and years before. As I said, it was not overt sin, but a matter of my habits and where I put my attention.

For example, you watch the television reports about people dying of cancer, or you attend a reunion where somebody talks about cancer, or people at work talk about their aunt who died of cancer. Soon, you are totally dominated by cancer and the fear of cancer. Then, years later, when the doctor says "cancer" to you, all of that fear suddenly rises up on the inside of you. That's where your doubt and unbelief come from.

Why does it happen? Because you considered something other than Jesus, the author and finisher of your faith. As Hebrews 12:3 says, *"For consider him that endureth such contradiction of sinners against himself, lest ye be wearied and faint in your minds."* There's that word "consider" again—it's everywhere!

The Curse of the Tube

What do we consider *most* in our society? It's probably television.

My mother is an educator who taught school for 42 years. She has seen surveys showing that children who watch television are something like *10 times* less creative than children who don't watch it. A child who doesn't watch television on a consistent basis can take a bolt and a nut and entertain himself for hours, but a child who has had television used as a babysitting tool can have a whole room full of toys and not have a thing to do! It destroys their creativity. Television is a powerful medium. Praise God that the gospel is finally making an impact on TV, but up until now, Satan has largely ruled it.

Television is so captivating that you don't even have to think to watch it. For example, you come home from work and you're dead tired. You turn on the boob tube so you can totally relax—it takes no effort on your part. There is no mental exercise; the producers can put your mind in the gutter whenever they want to. Even if there was nothing but gospel on television 24 hours a day, it would damage you to watch it, because you would be sitting there like a zombie letting someone else feed your mind.

Why are we tempted with so many things? It's because of the junk we consider.

Dr. Jesus

When my son, Joshua, was five or six years old, he asked me, "Daddy, what are doctors for?" He didn't know what a doctor was for! He didn't know there was any other option for healing than prayer. He had never *considered* it, because he'd never been taught it. I'm not against doctors, but God can heal you without a doctor—if you know how to tap into the healing power of God. Leave the doctors for people who believe they're sick! *I don't* believe I'm sick, even when it looks like I'm sick. I just don't relate to sickness. And so I've always been healed. I have doctors' reports to show I was healed of an incurable disease. I never have sickness, because I don't believe in it.

No Plan B

One of the reasons we get into trouble is because we entertain alternatives.

I don't have a Plan B or Plan C—it's only the gospel. Because of that, it works for me. One of the biggest hindrances to your faith is when you are *considering* something else (we can't seem to get away from that word). Satan will always push you to make a decision one way or the other. You can't have another plan in the wings and see it work. You must be single-minded on the Word of God.

I prayed for a lady once who had bad teeth. When I prayed for her, she told me that she already had made a dental appointment. Later, the Lord asked her, "Which way are you going to go? Are you going to believe me, or are you going to go to the dentist?" She thought about it and said, "God, I'm going to believe You. I don't care if my teeth rot out of my head." She called up and canceled the appointment, and by the time she hung up the phone, her teeth were completely healed!

Several days later, she came to me and asked, "Why did it happen at that time?" I said, "Because that's the first time you made a decision to believe God. Before, you still had a Plan B and C." She had considered something else.

Sadu Sundar Singh

We don't see nearly as many miracles in this country as they do in others. Let me give you an illustration of this.

A man named Sadu Sundar Singh was a legend in India in the early 1900s. If you mention his name there, people begin talking about all the miracles that happened. This man was a Moslem who was converted to Christ. He saw many people healed; in Bombay, for example, he saw as many as 100,000 people healed in a single day. He would go into a city and empty all the morgues, raising dozens of people from the dead. It was phenomenal. Singh finally had to stop praying for people because nobody would listen to him preach—they just thronged him to get at the healing power of God.

Singh saw tremendous things happen in India, but in the United States, it was a totally different story. Because of the expense of travel, Singh had planned a year-and-a-half tour of the U.S. After sailing over by ship in 1910, he got off the boat in New York City and spent 30 minutes walking around the city. Then he promptly canceled his speaking engagements, got back on the ship, and said, "I'll never preach to these people. They're so hard-hearted, they're so busy, they'll never hear it." And he went back to India.

He knew that where people are as preoccupied as we are with other things, the gospel would never penetrate. That was in 1910!

No News is Good News

Smith Wigglesworth knew the value of staying preoccupied with God.

A man went to visit him one time. When he knocked on his door, Smith said, "I'll let you in, but your newspaper has to stay outside." Smith couldn't read when he was first born again. He asked God to help him, and the Bible was the only book he ever read. He never read a newspaper or any other book in all his life.

A friend of mine in Colorado Springs had Smith Wigglesworth in her home when she was a child and told me her impressions of him. He carried his own communion elements and got up at four or five o'clock every morning to take communion and study the Word. After his wife died, he never spent 30 minutes without praying or studying the word. My friend said they never finished a meal without Smith stopping to have a Bible study. Their meals were usually cold, because he never stopped long enough to eat a whole meal without studying the Word.

Maybe you think that's a little strict, and perhaps it is. I read newspapers on occasion, and I've gotten some good things out of them for my preaching. I believe Smith Wigglesworth, in the course of 35 years, probably missed a dozen good things in the newspaper, things that could have benefited him, but he probably missed two or three hundred thousand bad things that would have made him fearful, preoccupied and sensitive to the world—things that would have put him back in touch with so-called reality, instead of the reality of God's Word. It would have affected his ministry for the worse.

It Takes Commitment

If all you did was meditate on God's Word day and night, then you would make *your* way prosperous and have good success; there's no alternative. You'd have a miracle ministry that would blow people's minds. You'd see the power of God operate in your life more than you ever thought possible. It doesn't take huge faith, but it does take pure faith.

We need to be sensitive to God, and we do that by the things we *consider*—what we focus our attention upon. Every person who has been greatly used of God was a fanatic in the matter of being separated from the world. You can love God and be carnal, but it's going to cost you your effectiveness. God's grace is always consistent, so He still loves you; but when you consider something other than Jesus, you deaden yourself to the voice of God, and you open yourself to the voice of the enemy.

Accepting Corruption

The reason most of us hear the devil easier than we do God is because we spend more time listening to the devil. Satan comes in insidious ways. Fifty years ago, for example, adultery and divorce were not nearly as common as they are today. Why are they being tolerated today? Satan has corrupted us in this area, and the biggest inroad he has used is television. Some of the old black-and-white comedies we consider to be clean, for example, actually hardened our hearts—they portrayed adultery or theft in a comic way and made fun of it. They took the seriousness out of it.

Christians weren't smart enough to realize it, so they started laughing at it, just like everybody else. The Bible says it's a shame to even *speak* of what the ungodly do in secret, so it lost its shame. The next step was to show somebody actually getting trapped in adultery (although they didn't really want it, understand), so that you would pity the person. It was still condemned as wrong, but the excuse was, "the devil made me do it," as Flip Wilson says. Today, it is virtually *glorified*, and some people think you're crazy for staying with one person all your life. There is a sitcom that even shows a man living with two girls! It's deteriorated to the point of total perversion.

Then we wonder why the Word of God is not producing in us. We're entertaining thoughts that God hates. We're crusting our hearts over. Some of you watch shows that feature homosexuality. Every time you persist in it— every time you laugh at homosexuality—you harden your heart toward God and His standards. Even shows that are considered harmless can make you hard-hearted: all that violence, immorality and perversion are totally opposed to God's nature. They should not be laughed at.

Shalt Thou Kill?

The same thing is true in the area of violence. Before I went to Vietnam, I was on an Army rifle range one day firing bullets at human-shaped targets, and it suddenly dawned on me that this wasn't cops and robbers. They were training me to *kill a man* made in the image of God. I can't tell you the feeling that came over me. I began to pray, "God, please help me never to kill a man." I am not necessarily a dove, or a hawk, on the subject of war. I believe that fighting is sometimes necessary, but I don't want to kill a man.

It occurred to me then, that when I was a kid, I played Hopalong Cassidy. I had two six-guns and rode a stick horse around all day. If my kids ever played with guns like they were killing someone, they were in big trouble with me. I let them play if they pretended to kill an animal and eat it, because God sanctioned that, but if they played like they were killing a man, they had my wrath to contend with! Someone might say, "But, Brother, that's just normal." It is normal for a corrupted, ungodly world, but God never intended for us to enjoy pretending we're killing people. However, the vast majority of good, well-meaning Christians have bought guns for their children just like everyone else.

Then we wonder why they're so violent. We wonder why they scream, "I'm going to kill you!" when another kid takes their toys away. We've let them play like they're killing a million people a day, so they're deadening themselves to the voice of God. It's no wonder violence finds such a natural place in kids today.

John Lake—A Driving Force for God

Let's look at another example of being separated to God: John Lake.

Lake was a mighty, powerful man of God in the early part of this century. He saw well over 500,000 *documented* cases of healing. He was licensed by the state of Washington as a medical doctor, although he had no medical training, because he saw so many people healed. He opened a hospital and had a staff of people that anointed patients with oil, prayed for them, and saw them healed. He even saw numerous people raised from the dead.

Like Smith Wigglesworth, John Lake was separated and sensitive to God. Once, he was driving up a mountain in Washington. As he was rounding a hairpin curve, the voice of the Lord suddenly said to him, "Pull over to the left-hand side of the road and park." Lake immediately pulled over to the left, which of course, isn't good on a left-hand curve going up a mountain! In a few seconds, a lumber truck came down the road out of control, nearly running off the road—it would have knocked John Lake off a 3,000-foot cliff. The only reason he was alive was because he was sensitive to the voice of God.

God is no respecter of persons. If God spoke to John Lake, He'll speak to you and me, but you and I aren't always listening. You and I have had our spiritual receiver tuned to something else. I would probably have responded to something like that about 30 minutes later, after I'd tested it a dozen ways. After it was too late.

John Lake was driving in a car with some people another time, when all of a sudden he just yelled, "Stop!" The fellow driving the car pulled over and asked, "What's wrong?" John Lake prayed, "God, forgive us. We've talked for 10 minutes and haven't even mentioned your name." He repented, asked God to forgive them, and they began talking about Jesus. That's the caliber of his commitment to a separated life.

Sensitive to God

It's no coincidence that men like John Lake and Smith Wigglesworth saw things happen that you and I haven't. They didn't have as much knowledge as we have, but they were totally sensitive to the knowledge they did have. It worked a thousand times better for them because their minds were stayed upon God. They didn't fill themselves with the junk of this world. I'm not saying this to condemn anyone, but to enlighten our eyes that we're polluting ourselves with doubt and unbelief. The Bible says, *"The light of the body is the eye: if therefore thine eye be single, thy whole body shall be full of light"* (Mt. 6:22). In other words, if you fill yourself with the Word of God, the Word of God will come out of you.

This principle works with anything, even things we don't consider to be sin. If I have one weakness, it's the Road Runner cartoon. I like the Road Runner—and it's not wrong to watch it—but if I get in trouble and out comes "beep beep," I've had it. I guarantee you, it won't heal my body, restore my marriage, or bolster my finances. It doesn't have to be an X-rated movie that nullifies the power of God in us. It can be anything other than God.

Separate Yourself Unto God

We have to start spending quality and quantity time with God, being separated unto Him. I dare you to spend a week shut off from the world, alone with God's Word, and see what it will do to you. It's impossible for you not to see results.

We also need to assemble together as a body and sit under the Word. That is a concept we put into practice at our campmeetings, which is why many people receive more there than they do anywhere else. We remove them from the things Satan has been using to feed them with doubt and unbelief. They don't have radio or television. They don't have pressures on a job. They don't have anyone striving with them. All they have is people speaking the Word of God, praising God, encouraging them, and talking about faith. People who are never touched under any other circumstances often have their lives totally changed at our campmeetings. They can do *anything* for God by the end of the week, because they've been fed the Word of God all week long and were separated from their natural surroundings. They're powerhouses of faith. We literally starved the devil out of them.

Whatever you are today is what you've been thinking yesterday. Proverbs 23:7 says, *"For as he [a man] thinketh in his heart, so is he. . . ."* Likewise, 2 Peter 1:3 says, *"According as his divine power hath given unto us all things that pertain unto life and godliness, through the knowledge of him that called us to glory and virtue. . . ."* Notice that these things come through knowledge. What kind of knowledge have you been meditating on? Whatever your life is, is a result of what you've been thinking.

Someone may object, "But I've really been in the Word and I still don't have it." But, as every farmer knows, when you plant corn in the ground, you get corn. When you plant soybeans, you get soybeans. When you plant weeds, you get weeds! It's an irrevocable law of God—

whatever you sow, that you will also reap (Gal. 6:7). If you're reaping depression, you've sowed depression. If you're reaping sickness, you've sowed sickness. If you're reaping poverty, you've sowed poverty, or at least you have allowed it through neglect. One way or another, you've allowed Satan to conquer you. You may say, "But I haven't been thinking I want to be sick." Maybe not, but your thinking has been sick. You may not have been thinking, "I want to be poor," but your thinking has been poor.

Isaac Polendo—On Fire for God

In Africa, around the turn of the century, there was a man named Isaac Polendo. His father was the witch doctor in their village and Isaac, even from a very young age, knew in his heart that witchcraft was wrong. He cried out for God, the true God, to reveal Himself to him. He had a dream in which he saw a white man come to his village and tell them about God (Isaac had never seen a white man before). He waited his entire life for this white man to come. Finally, a Presbyterian missionary came to the village and Isaac went to listen to him. He heard the gospel, but he thought it was the dumbest thing he'd ever heard: the missionary didn't present it in power and authority. But because of his vision, he stayed around the missionary. Finally, Isaac Polendo got saved. He was convinced it was real, but he knew very little about it.

The missionary tried to put him through the Presbyterian school and teach him how to read the Bible, but Isaac flunked. The missionaries said he was uneducable, so they wouldn't allow him to continue in school. Disillusioned, he went back to his hut and began to get drunk on coconut wine. He did virtually nothing with his faith. Some time later, when his wife was dying, he began to get really serious and asked God, "Why is this happening?" God appeared to him in a vision again and told him some great and mighty things. Inspired, Isaac laid hands on his wife and she was healed. He cut down his coconut grove, and went to re-enroll in school. In six weeks, he graduated from the school. God had totally turned his life and mind around.

Those Presbyterians still thought he would never amount to anything, so they just gave him a copy of the Bible and said, "Go back and read it, and whatever it says, do it." So he spent six months studying the Bible, then went to the next village and began preaching. He would sit in front of a hut, beat on a large drum, and the villagers would assemble to hear him. The witch doctor disliked him, so he started fighting against him, saying that he would curse anyone who came to the meetings. The crowd started dwindling, and finally no one came at all. To make matters worse, they put the drum Isaac used for his meetings in the middle of a large clearing, and used it for an orgy honoring their gods.

Angered, Isaac walked out into the middle of the clearing and prayed. A fire from heaven fell down and burned up the clearing. Isaac went out and got his drum, put it in front of his hut and began beating it. The whole village came to hear him and got saved. Then he went to the next village. Word spread, people came and got healed and delivered. The witch doctor in that village came against him. When the chief's wife was dying, the witch doctor said, "This man who preaches this strange God is the problem." Isaac kept on preaching. Finally, the chief's wife died. When that happened, the people all came to kill Isaac, but just before they did, he said, "Wait a minute." He walked into the chief's hut, raised his wife from the dead and walked back out with her. The chief and his entire village got saved.

Isaac went to the next village, and the chief there had two sons crippled with clubfoot. He prayed for them, they were instantly healed, and the chief made the whole village come and get saved. Isaac went back and told the missionaries what had happened and they said, "No, no, God doesn't do those kinds of miracles anymore!" But they were too late; it had already happened.

This example reveals that if we weren't polluted with so much doubt and unbelief, God would do anything through us. We could see everything Isaac did, and what the missionaries failed to do.

What About You?

If God can save you, He can accomplish anything in your life. You don't have to know all kinds of great theological truths if you'd just focus on what you do know. You can remove all of the debris of doubt and unbelief that has been sown in your life by humbling yourself, repenting, and letting God cleanse you. If you've spent 20, 30 or 40 years absorbing doubt and unbelief, praise God that it doesn't have to take another 20 or 30 years to get it out, because God's power will cleanse you of it now.

In 2 Corinthians 10:4-5, it says *"(For the weapons of our warfare are not carnal, but mighty through God to the pulling down of strong holds); Casting down imaginations, and every high thing that exalteth itself against the knowledge of God, and bringing into captivity every thought to the obedience of Christ;"* Perhaps you're thinking, *But I can't keep my mind stayed on God all the time.* Yes, you can. You can bring into captivity *every* thought to the obedience of Jesus; the Bible says so. It's a lie from the devil that you can't control your mind.

All of us have had times when we worried all day, and yet performed on our jobs and did other daily tasks. Worry is simply keeping our minds stayed on the negative things in our lives. If we can worry all day, we can keep our minds stayed on God's Word all day (2 Cor. 3:3-5).

You can control your mind at home. You can control it at church. You can control it on the job. I know—I controlled it in Vietnam! You may not be able to stop the source, but doubt and unbelief do not have to penetrate you; they don't have to rule you. You do not have to be dominated by natural, worldly things. You can reverse it, and it all starts by focusing your attention on Jesus. Consider Jesus, and He will dominate you.

Part 3:
The Cure

The cure for a hardened heart is a total commitment to keep our minds stayed on the Lord.

5

Stop the Conception

As I said before, some people think temptation is nearly automatic, that a certain part of us is just bent on sin, but that's not so. There is nothing within you that *makes* you sin. It is your nature, according to Galatians 5:22-23, to operate in love, joy, peace, longsuffering, gentleness, goodness, faith, meekness, and temperance. That is normal for Christians. The reason other things enter is because we entertain contrary thoughts.

Sin has to be conceived, just as a child has to be conceived. If you stop the conception, then you don't have to fight such a strong battle when sin presents itself.

Many Christians, however, wait until the battle is raging, then try to summon up faith, rebuke the devil, use the name of Jesus, and overcome temptation. There is a better way—stop the temptation before it starts. If we neglect the Word of God, if we neglect time with the Lord, we will be hardened towards the Lord, but if we neglect the devil, we will find that it is not easy to hear the voice of the devil. We can stop that temptation in its tracks.

My First Baptist Healing

I remember the first person I ever saw healed. I was teaching a Baptist Sunday School class. I didn't know that God healed back then, but I read in the Word that *"...they shall lay hands on the sick, and they shall recover"* (Mk. 16:18).

I began reading that verse to my class, a group of high school students, every Sunday. I said, "I know this isn't what the Baptists teach, and I've never seen it, but it's in God's Word, so we're going to lay hands on the sick and they will recover. If you get sick, don't stay away from church. We'll lay hands on you."

One day a girl named Diane came in sick. She was so sick she was actually green! When I saw her, my first reaction was, "What are you doing here?" She said, "Well, you said if I was sick I should come and have you lay hands on me." I swallowed hard and said, "Well, that's what the Word says." We sat her down in a chair and prayed, but she looked worse rather than better. I resumed teaching the class. Finally, she got so sick she had to go home.

Later I went into the church service, feeling really defeated. I said, "God, I did exactly what You said to the best of my ability. Why didn't it work?" During the song service, I looked around, and that girl was in the back of the church, frantically waving at me. I went back there, and she said, "By the time I got home I was totally healed!" We interrupted the service and made an announcement to that *whole* Baptist church that this girl was healed!

I was as surprised as anybody to see her healed, but that's the way I was when I started out ministering. Every time I laid hands on somebody, I'd wonder, *God, is this going to work?* Because of that, we saw some healed, and some not healed.

Arthritis Pain—Gone!

Over the years, however, I've renewed myself in that area. For example, take arthritis: I have great faith that I can make *anybody's* arthritic pain leave, whether they're believers or not, because I've exercised my faith in that area.

Once, for example, we had a miracle service in Childress, Texas. A lady came to the meeting. She was on a walker, and was shuffling around, almost totally paralyzed from arthritis. She came forward and *I knew that I knew* she was going to get healed, so I laid hands on her. I prayed, grabbed her hands, and said, "Let's walk." She said, "Oh, I can't walk, brother." And I said, "Yes, you can." She said, "No, I can't," and so I pulled on her a little bit. Finally I leaned her forward and began to let go. She started shuffling *fast*. Finally, she cried, "Oh, it hurts," but I was hardened toward what the devil had to say. So I said, "I don't care if it hurts. We're going to walk."

She walked all around that place. It took her 30 minutes to walk from the back door and sit down, but before she left she was well enough to leave her walker inside.

Then she called me the next week; all of her pain had come back. So I went to her house and told her, "God healed you and the Bible says the gifts and the callings of God are without repentance, according to Romans 11:29." I prayed over her again and her pain left. Then she'd call the next week; her pain was back. For a year and-a-half, I exercised myself that way, making her pain leave, but she wasn't operating in faith.

That may not have been the best way to minister to her, but it was great for me! I saw that I had authority over arthritis.

Arthritis Knuckles Under Again

Another lady in Childress came in, who was given less than 24 hours to live, by the doctors. She didn't tell me what her sickness was, and that was good, because our eyes, our senses, will hinder us unless they're under control. I was standing in front of the church with my eyes closed, singing and playing the guitar. When I asked people to come forward, I didn't see that her friends literally had to carry her up there. When she got up there I said, "Give me your hands."

I still had my eyes closed. God literally had to turn my senses off for this thing to work!

I prayed for her, put her hands up in the air, and said, "Now, do something you couldn't do." She screamed, and I asked, "What's the matter?" She said, "I haven't lifted my hands in eight years!" I said, "You haven't? Well, do something else you couldn't do." She began walking back and forth. I asked, "You haven't walked?" She said, "Not in over eight years." I asked her what was wrong, and she showed me her hands. They were terribly gnarled—the fingers were actually at right angles to the hands. She had literally been on her deathbed for months. Within two weeks, her hands were completely normal. A specialist examined her and told her, "Lady, I know what your record says, but you have *never* had arthritis."

Because of those incidents, I can pray for arthritis today, and it will leave.

A Special Anointing?

I have no special anointing for arthritis—God gave me just as much power over any other sickness and disease as arthritis, but that's an area in which I've exercised my faith. God gave us power over *all* the power of the enemy (Lk. 10:19). If you have a special anointing to see legs grow, for example, it's because you've exercised yourself in that area.

Most of us have faith for certain areas. But it's a lie from the devil that you have to have doubt and unbelief in other areas. You don't. You can renew your mind and eliminate the vast majority of Satan's warfare against you. You can *stop the conception.*

Someone might say, "But, Brother, you're a preacher. It's easy for you to say that—you stay around Christians all the time and don't have to contact the world."

You've never been a preacher if you believe that! You should have the responsibility, the worry and the pressures a preacher has for a while. It's not easy to serve God. You put yourself on the front lines, responsible for a thousand people in a church, and see what kind of trouble the devil gives you.

Facing the Music in Vietnam

When I went through Vietnam, I lived with the doubt and unbelief of others 24 hours a day, and I saw myself victorious in every situation—but not without effort.

The thing I hated worst in Vietnam was the ungodly music. I was the lowest ranking man in my bunker, but I determined that I wasn't going to listen to that music, or the blaspheming and cursing God all the time. I got a poster board and a marker and wrote Exodus 20:7 in big letters on it. I hung it on the wall so that when anyone opened the door, the first thing they saw was: *"Thou shalt not take the name of the Lord thy God in vain; for the Lord will not hold him guiltless that taketh his name in vain."*

From that time on, not another cussword was said. For three months not a single word was said to me of any kind! They stopped playing the radios and left the bunker to drink. They didn't even acknowledge that I was there. You might think that was bad, but it was better than hearing all of their filth and perversion.

A Militant Faith

When I was in the United States before being shipped out to Vietnam, I was held over at a base. One day, we were waiting to get paid, and were down in this little stairway that was no larger than 10 by 10 feet. There were about 40 people huddled down there, trying to stay out of the cold and wind. None of them knew me. They were cursing and blaspheming God, just like soldiers do. There was a tall fellow there, named David, who was a former gospel singer before he was drafted. He was not living for God, and was blaspheming the Lord and making jokes about Christians, just like everyone else. Finally, he got a twinge of conviction, and said, "That's no way for a good-ole Scofield-carrying Baptist to talk."

I asked, "You have a Scofield Bible?" And he said, "Yeah, do you?" And I said, "I sure do. Why don't you ever read yours?" And he said, "What do you mean, ever read mine?" I said, "Have you ever read Matthew 12:36?" And he said, "I don't know what it says." And I said, "It says, '...*every idle word that men shall speak, they shall give account thereof in the day of judgment. For by thy words thou shalt be justified, and by thy words thou shalt be condemned.*'"

Boy! He got mad and began pushing his way through that crowd, and just as he got up to me, I said, "One other scripture—Galatians 4:16 says, *'Am I therefore become your enemy, because I tell you the truth?'*" He just stood there glaring at me, then turned around and walked away. He didn't say anything, and for the next 30 minutes, *no one* said anything! Again, I didn't have to listen to all their doubt and unbelief. Two-and-a-half months later, that fellow got right with God, and told me that he had been under such conviction, he hadn't slept a wink since then.

The very first night I was in the Army, everybody was cursing and blaspheming God in the barracks. It was night and the lights were out. Suddenly one guy said, "Even though I talk this way, I really do know God." I said, "Did you ever read 1 John?" He said, "Who said that?" I said, "In 1 John 2:4, it says, *'He that saith, I know him, and keepeth not his commandments, is a liar, and the truth is not in him.'*" He got mad, turned the lights on, and started walking around, saying, "Who said that?" I just acted like I was asleep. I never said a word. *They* never said a word—they all went to sleep. It worked.

What About You?

How does this apply to you? Suppose people at work are running down the President of the United States. We know the President is the ruler of our people, and we're commanded to pray for him; but people criticize him constantly, and that's negative. It hardens your heart toward God because you're violating the Word of God. Psalm 1:1 says, *"Blessed is the man that walketh not in the counsel of the ungodly, nor standeth in the way of sinners, nor sitteth in the seat of the scornful."* What should you do? You don't have to criticize *them*, but you can say, "According to Romans 13:1-4, the President is the ruler of my people, ordained by God for my good, and I've been praying for him." Do you know what will happen? Either those people will repent, or they will never mention it around you again. In either case, you win.

At church, in the Army, on the job—anyplace you find yourself—you can stop the conception. That's half the battle.

6

Understanding Unbelief

L et's review for a moment. We've learned that
our hearts can be hardened. Having a hard heart
is defined as being deprived of wisdom, judgment and
understanding (Mk. 8:17-19). The way your heart be-
comes hardened is by *what you do not consider* (Mk.
6:52). What you focus your attention on, you'll be sensitive to; what you neglect, you'll be hardened to. Most of
us have neglected the things of God and paid attention to
the things of the world.

"Because of your unbelief..."

In Matthew, chapter 17, there is a perfect example
of a hardened heart. Jesus' disciples are trying to cast a
demon out of a boy. Starting at verse 14, it says, *"And*

when they were come to the multitude, there came to him a certain man, kneeling down to him, and saying, Lord, have mercy on my son: for he is lunatic, and sore vexed: for ofttimes he falleth into fire, and oft into the water. And I brought him to thy disciples, and they could not cure him. Then Jesus answered and said, O faithless and perverse generation, how long shall I be with you? how long shall I suffer you? bring him hither to me. And Jesus rebuked the devil; and he departed out of him: and the child was cured from that very hour. Then came the disciples to Jesus apart, and said, Why could not we cast him out? And Jesus said unto them, Because of your unbelief. . . . "

If I asked you, "Why have *you* prayed for something and not seen the manifestation?" the typical answer would be: "Not enough faith." Jesus' disciples asked Him the same question, "Why couldn't we cast him out?" Jesus didn't say they didn't have enough faith. Instead, He pointed to their unbelief.

Faith and Unbelief

You can have faith and unbelief at the same time. Most people have never considered this. They think you either have faith or unbelief, but not a mixture of the two.

For instance, Jesus once said, *"Be not afraid, only believe"* (Mk. 5:36). Why didn't He just say "believe"? It's because it's possible to believe and disbelieve at the same time. Also, a man once told Jesus, *"Lord, I believe; help thou my unbelief"* (Mk. 9:24). In other words, the man said, "I have faith, but I have unbelief at the same time." Mark 11:23 says, *"For verily I say unto you, That whosoever shall say unto this mountain, Be thou removed, and be thou cast into the sea; and shall not doubt in his heart, but shall believe that those things which he saith shall come to pass; he shall have whatsoever he saith."* Why would Jesus say, *"and shall not doubt"* if faith is automatically the absence of doubt? It's because you can operate in faith and unbelief at the same time.

This has been a source of confusion to many people, because they've seen their faith work, but when they *don't* see it work, they ask, "God, what's wrong? I know I prayed in faith. I've seen it work before, and now it doesn't seem to be working." The problem is that you had faith, but it was hindered by unbelief.

Hold Your Horses

Here is an example. You can hook a team of horses up to a weight and exert tremendous power in one direction. Under normal circumstances, it would move. But if you had a team of horses pulling in the opposite direction at the same time, exerting equal force, the net effect would be zero. In the same way, a lot of us really do release our faith, but it is negated by unbelief. Nothing moves.

When Jesus rebuked the disciples, He didn't say, "You don't have any faith." He said, "It's because of your unbelief." Remember, in Matthew, chapter 10, the disciples had already been commissioned with power over unclean spirits, and over *all* sickness and disease. They had seen people delivered, apparently *every* person delivered. They didn't ask, "Jesus, why wasn't this one cast out?" They didn't believe that miracles had passed away the night before, like some people believe today!

They knew about faith, but they still didn't see results. I've had that same problem, and I've wondered, *God, I've seen it work so easily before—why isn't it working now?* It's because of unbelief.

Mountain-Stopping Unbelief

In Matthew 17:20, Jesus continues rebuking the disciples: *"for verily I say unto you, If ye have faith as a grain of mustard seed, ye shall say unto this mountain, Remove hence to yonder place; and it shall remove; and nothing shall be impossible unto you."* Imagine that: faith the size of a mustard seed is enough to cast a mountain into the sea! In other words, the faith we had to get born again is enough to see anything happen. It's enough to see cancer healed. It's enough to see people delivered. It's enough to see the dead raised . . . *if* it's not mixed with unbelief.

Many people try to build faith, build faith, build faith—and that's not totally wrong, but they don't deal with their unbelief. Some of us have such high levels of unbelief that the only way we'll ever receive anything is through corporate faith: we'll always have to have the entire church pray for us.

The only consistent way to live in victory is to decrease your unbelief level, to just pull the plug on unbelief. If you do that, you'll find that *"with his stripes we are healed"* (Isa. 53:5) is all you need to maintain total healing. You won't need a thousand scriptures on healing; one will do . . . *if* you don't have any unbelief to wipe it out.

What is Unbelief?

Unbelief can take various forms. It can be total rebellion, such as saying, "I just don't believe this, even though it's scripture." That's unbelief. Or it can also be as small as saying, "I believe God heals, but what if. . . ?"

The Bible says in James 1:5-8, *"If any of you lack wisdom, let him ask of God, that giveth to all men liberally, and upbraideth not; and it shall be given him. But let him ask in faith, nothing wavering."* Again, this is an example of belief and unbelief occurring at the same time. *"For he that wavereth is like a wave of the sea driven with the wind and tossed. For let not that man think that he shall receive any thing of the Lord. A double minded man [is] unstable in all his ways."* The Bible talks a lot about being single-minded. That means don't believe and disbelieve at the same time. Confessing the Word, believing that you're healed, but then questioning God when a pain hits you, is unbelief.

What You See is What You Get

In Mark 9:20, the Bible cites the same instance of the disciples and the lunatic boy. It says, *"And they brought him unto him: and when he saw him, straightway the spirit tare him; and he fell on the ground, and wallowed foaming."* This demon, in other words, had a *physical* manifestation. The disciples saw it.

It's easier to release your faith for something you *don't* see, as I did for the lady with arthritis. This is why it's so hard, for example, for people to get their eyes healed.

Your eyes are your strongest sensory knowledge gate. Over 80 percent of your contact with the physical world comes through your eyes. You depend more upon them than what you feel, hear, smell or taste—all combined. When someone has hands laid on him for his eyes to be healed, immediately his eyes either say, "You're healed," or "You're not healed." If that healing is not instantaneous, that person is in for the fight of his life. Most Christians have never learned how to bring their senses into subjection, so most of them fail to get their eyes healed, even though it takes no more faith to heal your eyes than it does to heal your big toe! If there is no instantaneous manifestation, there will be more unbelief to deal with concerning your eyes than there would be concerning your big toe.

The disciples *saw* this demon convulse this boy, and it's my personal opinion that when they saw it, they related easier to the physical manifestation than they did to their faith. That's where their unbelief came from.

Is Unbelief Normal?

Many people believe that this is perfectly normal; that our emotions *must* go contrary to the Word. They say, "Well, it's just human. You'll always have fears. You'll always have doubts." I will admit this: because none of us are where we're supposed to be, we do experience these things, but it is wrong to think we have to. Hebrews 5:14 says, *"But strong meat belongeth to them that are of full age, even those who by reason of use have their senses exercised to discern both good and evil."* Our physical senses—what we see, taste, hear, smell, and feel—are what this is talking about. It says we can literally bring them into subjection, bring them to the point that they don't always have to be going contrary to God.

I was raised in a denomination that taught if you wanted to know God's will, take your first reaction and do the opposite. That may be true for a carnal Christian (the carnal mind is enmity against God, according to Romans 8:7), but we don't have to stay that way! We can change. Instead of thinking, *Oh, no, what's going to happen if I lay hands on this person and they're not healed?* we can get to the point where we say, "Satan, what are you going to do when I lay hands on them and they are healed?" You can look on the positive side of it. You can change your emotions and be receptive to the things of God.

In other words, we can exercise our senses to the point that they will be sensitized to God more than to the world, more than to the junk on television, more than to sin, hatred, strife, unbelief, jealousy and adultery. Our emotions do not always have to be unbridled, but most Christians' emotions are unbridled because they've never disciplined themselves and brought them into subjection. That's a tremendous hindrance to their faith.

I believe that was the disciples' problem. It wasn't that they disbelieved God; they had a lot of faith. They had seen God work and they had seen their faith produce, but they had not brought their emotions, their senses, into line. So when they encountered a negative situation they were simply moved by it—not moved far, but far enough so they couldn't cast that demon out.

Finally, in Matthew 17:21, Jesus said, *"Howbeit this kind goeth not out but by prayer and fasting."* That's what we'll consider next.

7

The Role of Prayer and Fasting

In this chapter, we'll look at how prayer and fasting fit in with hardness of heart.

Mark, chapter 9, covers the same incident as Matthew, chapter 17, where the disciples tried and failed to expel the demon from the epileptic boy. In verse 29, Jesus tells them, *"This kind can come forth by nothing, but by prayer and fasting."*

Because of that verse, many of us have erroneously thought that some demons are so strong that even the name of Jesus won't get them out: we have to add prayer and fasting. That's not good theology. Every demon ever created trembles at the name of Jesus.

Why Prayer and Fasting?

So why should we engage in prayer and fasting?

Prayer and fasting doesn't move the devil and it doesn't move God. God had *already* given the disciples all power in heaven and earth, according to Luke 10:19. They didn't have to fast and pray for a double anointing or anything like that. It is possible for us to operate in twice the anointing we've operated in before, but it's because we're learning how to release what God has given us, not because He gives us more. When God called us, He gave us all the anointing we'll ever get.

Fasting and prayer won't move God. What fasting and prayer does is affect your senses, to bring them into line so that, for example, when you see a boy falling on the ground, wallowing and foaming, you don't immediately think, *It didn't work. God didn't heal him.* You've brought your senses into subjection so they'll respond to your spirit, and your spirit dictates to them instead of them dictating to your spirit.

Moving God's "Pity Bone"?

When some of us don't see our prayers work, we ask, "God, why haven't you moved yet? I've done everything. What does it take?" No answer. So we think, *Well, I'm going to fast, and when I waste away and become really pathetic, then God will see how sincere I am and He'll move on my behalf.* In essence, we use a fast to change God. God has already moved by grace—we don't have to move Him. It is *ourselves* we're moving by fasting and prayer. If God isn't already on our side by what Jesus did, our fasting and prayer is not going to add the finishing touch!

I've heard people say, "I've done everything I know, and I'm going to fast until God heals me." Well, you're going to waste away then; you're going to go hungry.

Weighed Down with. . .Weight!

We need to fast because of carnality, not to move God. We can look at our lives and see areas of carnality where our body and our senses have been dictating to us. Most of us can turn sideways in the mirror and see more than enough evidence to prove that our body dictates to us!

If you can't control your eating, you'll also have trouble when you try to release your faith. Suppose you pray for healing. Your body says, "I must not be healed; I still hurt." And you say, "Shut up, body, we're going to believe God." And your body says, "Who are you to tell me to shut up? You don't control me in any other area. Do you think you're going to control me now?" Your body, your senses, have to be *"exercised to discern both good and evil"* (Heb. 5:14). That doesn't happen automatically. Don't think you're going to be able to overcome that body if you never discipline it, never train it, never control it. If you're like most people, your body has been spoiled rotten and it's not in any mood to knuckle under and do what you tell it to.

Train Up a Child. . .Your Body!

Take children for example. When our children go to church, they sit through the service quietly and don't move.

They listen; they pay attention. People ask us, "How can your children sit through a two or three hour service and not misbehave?" These same people bring their own kids to church and watch them fight, struggle and squirm the whole time, and they wonder why.

Their kids have been taught all their lives to be hyper—they've never been taught to be still a day in their lives. Some people think, *Well, it's just normal for a child to be that way.* That's *not* normal. When our children were young, we always made them take a nap or have a rest time, where they sat for at least an hour. If they didn't go to sleep, they read a book, studied the Bible, or prayed; we trained them to be still, and they loved it. The Bible says, *"Be still, and know that I [am] God. . ."* (Ps. 46:10). There is a whole generation of people today who've not learned to be still—they literally go berserk if they don't have all their time occupied with something such as television, radio or the movies.

We're missing one of the greatest blessings in life if we don't take time to be still and know that He is God.

Throw a Fit and Get It

Did you ever see a little kid throw a fit? The parents say, "Now you be quiet." The kid starts screaming, "I want that!" Do you know what most parents do? Get "that" and give it to him, to shut him up; so the child thinks to himself, *Boy, that'll work. If I ever want anything, I'll throw a fit and I'll get it.* Then the parents wonder why the kid throws fits all the time. It's because they reward him every time he does it.

Our bodies are the same way. How can we expect them to reject what they feel and operate in faith when they have never been taught to reject anything? Our bodies have been indulged. If it wants something, feed it! If you do that, I guarantee that your body will dictate to you rather than you dictating to it, because you reward it every time it lusts after something. It's just like a spoiled child.

Instead, you should say, "Body, you give me any more trouble and we're going on a 10-day fast." It screams, "Oh, no, I couldn't live through a 10-day fast." You answer, "It just went to 11 days." It screams, "Eleven days! I can't stand it." You answer, "I'll go to 12 if you don't shut up." Pretty soon, your body will get the message and shut up.

The Trouble with Fasting

Fasting can help you get discipline in your life, but let me warn you about a misconception concerning fasting.

You've probably heard a lot of people give great testimonies about fasting. They say, "Oh, I saw 10 angels, and three visions, and God visited me, and all kinds of great things happened." So somebody says, "I'm going to fast. I want to see three angels and 10 visions and all those other things." He goes on a fast, and it's miserable! His head hurts, his stomach growls, he complains, is irritable and says, "Boy, this isn't the 700 Club. I thought it was going to be great. I thought I was going to have these great supernatural visitations. What's wrong?" He backs off the fast.

Fasts that are supernaturally sustained are an unusual occurrence. Very seldom are you going to have angelic visitations. The average *good* fast is a fight. Why? Because your taste—that is, your lust for food—is one of your strongest drives. The Old Testament says that Esau sold his birthright for a mess of pottage! He lost all his reason and went completely berserk because of food.

Up Comes Carnality!

Food is not bad nor is the desire for it—the Bible says so; but if it totally dominates you, it's wrong, and a fast will bring your carnality to the surface in a hurry. You can read and meditate on the Word, go to church, and pray for months or even years to get your body under control, but a fast will bring it to a life or death crisis in one or two days' time. When it gets to the point that you're going berserk, you may say, "This is terrible. I'm not getting blessed." But you are! Every bit of carnality that has been ruling you—probably without your even realizing it—has risen to the surface. Everything that is not submitted to God is raising its ugly head. Your emotions go wild: you get depressed, you get discouraged, you get irritable. You scream, "Boy, this isn't what I need!" but it's exactly what you need; you've brought every bit of trash in your life to the surface. You need to stay with it!

If you will *continue* that discipline after the fast, you can say, "Body, you will not rule me anymore. When I tell you to raise your hands, you're going to raise your hands. When I tell you to dance in front of people, you're going to dance in front of people, and not worry about what they think. When I tell you to stay up late and study the Word, you're going to say up late and study the Word, and not fall asleep. From now on, I'll dominate *you* instead of you dominating me."

Not by Bread Alone

The Word is also a tremendous help on a fast. When Jesus was tempted, He told the devil, *"Man shall not live by bread alone, but by every word that proceedeth out of the mouth of God"* (Mt. 4:4). Proverbs 4:22 says, *"For they [God's words] are life unto those that find them, and health to all their flesh."* The Word can actually give physical strength to you. On a prolonged fast, you can literally begin to draw nourishment from the Word. Stay in the Word on a fast.

However, if you're watching all the food advertisements on television—Burger King, McDonald's and Kentucky Fried Chicken—you won't last long. You'll have to unplug from all that and put your attention on God, and do you know what that will accomplish? It will harden you towards the things of the world. Your senses will begin going inward, to be exercised to discern both good and evil (Heb. 5:14).

Through prayer and fasting, you can reach the point that your senses don't have to lead you into doubt and unbelief. You'll be able to look at someone with an amputated arm or leg and not be immediately flooded with doubt and unbelief. You'll see through the eye of your faith, and that person will be healed! You can get to the point that your senses become a positive, productive thing rather than a negative, counterproductive thing.

But it's not going to happen accidentally—it's going to take *much* prayer and fasting.

What About Prayer?

So far, I have largely described fasting, because it's so powerful and so few of us do it! But now let's look at prayer.

Prayer does the same thing fasting does: it causes your natural man to rebel. It doesn't satisfy the senses; it forces them to get under control. Praying in tongues does so especially. When I first prayed in tongues, my mind rebelled at it. It said, "This is foolish; this is silly. What's the point?" *I prayed in tongues an hour a day for two years*, and fought that thought with everything I had. Finally I broke through. Now I can pray in tongues and I don't have those battles. I've exercised my senses.

Many times you say, "I'm going to spend time praying in tongues." You decide to pray for an hour, then five minutes later you're thinking about something else. Then you start looking at the clock. Finally, you give up. Why does that happen? The Bible says in Matthew 6:21, *"For where your treasure is, there will your heart be also."* Your treasure has been in the world and your heart will naturally gravitate to where your treasure is.

You can focus your attention on God so much that regardless of what you're doing, your mind always gravitates back to Him. I often wake up at night after preaching a service and think of people being healed, delivered and set free. I can't get away from it—I sleep it, I dream it, I talk it. That's what my mind is stayed on. That's where my heart is, so it's natural that I gravitate back to it again and again.

You Have it All

When you were born again, you received the same measure of faith Jesus had (Rom. 12:3, Gal. 2:20). You have all you can ever use or need. It's a simple matter of getting rid of the unbelief that hinders it.

That's not going to happen accidentally. It's going to happen by a deliberate attack on the things in our lives that Satan uses as inroads. It's going to happen by much prayer and fasting.

8

Concluding Thoughts

This teaching about hardness of heart has done a lot for me. I hope it has for you. Let me conclude with some final thoughts.

First, remember it is not your holiness that makes any of this work. I've heard all my life, "Live holy, live holy, live holy!" With this goes the idea that God won't bless you if you don't live holy, but that is false. If God waited until we were holy to bless us, none of us would ever get blessed. If you say, "Brother, I live holy," I'll ask you, "Who are you comparing yourself to? It must be some other human being. You can't be comparing yourself to God's standard, because you don't match up to that. God doesn't use you because of your holiness. God has never had anybody qualified working for Him yet—never.

It's not your holiness that moves God, but your holiness, your separation, and your commitment does determine how sensitive you are to God and how susceptible you are to Satan's doubt and unbelief. Sure, you can learn how to overcome doubt and unbelief, but it's a greater thing not to be tempted with them in the first place!

Single-Mindedness is the Key

Second, understand that you have to be single-minded. If you look at any person who has been mightily used of God, you'll find it wasn't because he was a great man of faith—it was because he was a *little* man of unbelief! I use the example of Abraham: he didn't know how to disbelieve God. His strength was that he was absolutely single-minded on God.

You can get so single-minded on something that you just don't know how to do anything else. For example, I have literally become a misfit. If I were to fail in the ministry now, I'd probably starve to death. I just don't know how to do anything else. I don't know how to respond to this world. I've found what God made me for; I'm doing it, and I don't have a plan B or plan C. I'm committed. My bridges are burned behind me. I'm convinced that this is one of the reasons my ministry is succeeding; Satan can't tell me, "You should quit and do something else." That isn't an option for me.

I've had lots of opportunities to quit the ministry, but it's not a temptation for me. Again, Hebrews 11:15 says, *"And truly, if they had been mindful of that country from whence they came out, they might have had oppor-*

tunity to have returned." Turn that around: because they were not mindful of the country they came out of, they could not be tempted to return. I'm not even tempted to go another direction because I don't consider any other options.

You Already Have Faith

Third, remember that it's not a matter of "getting more faith."

You already have faith. If you've been born again, you have faith. We know more about faith than any generation on the face of the earth has ever known, but we're doing less with it because we've become so weighed down with the things of this world, so obsessed with the luxuries America can produce. We're the most preoccupied generation of believers who has ever lived, a society inundated with facts, but very few of them about God.

We can turn on our television sets and see what is happening on the other side of the world in *real time*. That has never been available to any other society before. That has some great privileges, but it has a great responsibility too. We ought to be managing all that information, but most of us aren't. The networks certainly aren't managing it for us; if you're depending on them for news, you are misinformed and uninformed. It is slanted and bigoted. Yet most Christians listen to it and swallow it, just like everyone else.

We criticize the President, political candidates, the personalities in the news—just like everyone else. We've become sensitive to criticism and scorning, letting Satan come into our lives, and have become hardened towards the things of God, then we wonder why faith isn't working.

What is Your Priority?

What this teaching really centers on is a matter of priorities. Most of our priorities are way out of line with God's.

Consider tragedy for example. If somebody close to you dies, your immediate reaction is, "Boy, all the stuff that seemed important to me just isn't important anymore." The *people* around you suddenly become important. Your priorities fall into line. Suddenly, you become desensitized to the world. You reach out to God in a situation like that and may see one of the greatest miracles you've ever seen; but sadly, most of us go right back to our lifestyles when it's over, harden ourselves, and then wonder why it doesn't work again.

Most of us are crisis-oriented. Only when it's necessary do we do anything. For example, very few of us mow the grass when it can be done easily. We wait until it gets a foot high—an embarrassment to us and our neighbors—before we do it. We do the same thing with God. Most of us wait until there is a crisis before we call out to God. An *opportunity* is the most advantageous time to respond to God, not when it is a necessity. The people who really prosper with God are those who've learned to elevate opportunity to the status of necessity.

For example, most of us have been convicted about spending special time with God, but it's just not convenient; so we let it go until tragedy strikes. Then suddenly, all the things that were once so important just fall by the wayside, and we make time for God. It's a necessity for us to go to work, so some of us get up early in the morning to pray, but on Saturdays there's no necessity to get up early, so we don't spend that time with God. We should be like Job, who said, *". . .I have esteemed the words of his [God's] mouth more than my necessary food"* (Job 23:12).

It's Worth the Cost

You will do whatever you consider vital. Most of us haven't considered being separate from this world vital. Someone might say, "Brother, you're being a little strict— you don't have to be that way." I agree; you don't have to be that way. You can be a Christian and not be totally separated unto God, but I have decided that seeing people's lives changed—blind eyes opened, cancer healed, dead people raised, people born again and baptized in the Holy Ghost—is worth all my sacrifice. People come up to me, hug me and say, "Brother, if it weren't for you, I'd have been dead. . .our home would have been destroyed. . . I wouldn't have been born again." Those kind of things make it all worth it.

For example, I received a letter not long ago from a lady in prison . She's not eligible for parole for many years. She is born again, but she has been laboring under total condemnation and guilt. She was listening to our program on the radio. I was talking about ministering to the Lord and she asked, "God, what can I do here, in solitary confinement? Who can I bless?" She found out that the first call on any Christian's life is not to serve, but to minister to God, to give back the love He has given to us. She wrote me a letter, and it is one of the most powerful things I've ever read. She said, "Thank you. You reached me. Now I have something I can do. I can bless God. I can minister to Him. My whole life has changed. Now it doesn't seem like it's going to be so long in here because I have something to do."

It's worth it. It's worth turning off the television. I don't know all the football scores. I don't know all the baseball scores. I don't even know who won the World Series. It's not sin to know these things, but I didn't miss a thing by not knowing them. You may have missed a lot of things by knowing them.

Putting God first may cost you. It may cost you some of your time, some of your conveniences, some of your pleasures; but it will also cost you your strife, your sickness, your carnality—all the things that are destroying your life and making you depressed, frustrated and ineffective.

How Badly Do You Want to Succeed?

What I've shared in this teaching on hardness of heart is not great revelation, but it's practical; it will work. I challenge you to take what I've taught and implement it in your life—it will be *impossible* for you not to succeed. How badly do you want to succeed? If I guaranteed that my plan would make you a millionaire one year from this date, wouldn't you do what it takes? I can guarantee that if you operate 100 percent in what I have ministered in this book for one year, the entire world will know who you are! If you spent a solid year not letting doubt and unbelief into your life, doing nothing but letting faith reign, you would have a huge following of people whose lives would be changed.

If you want it badly enough, to do what the Word of God says—it's there.

It's simple. There is nothing hard about the gospel. It doesn't take a great mind. It doesn't take great finances. All it takes is a great commitment. It will change your life. I promise you that.

About the Author

Andrew was brought up in the Baptist denomination in a Christian home in Arlington, Texas. He made a total commitment of his life to the Lord at a very young age, but it wasn't until he received the baptism of the Holy Spirit as a teenager that he began to experience the power of God in his life.

Since that time, he has pastored three churches in progressive steps towards the ministry to which God has called him - teaching the body of Christ the "Good News" of our New Testament relationship in Jesus Christ.

Andrew is fulfilling this call as he travels throughout the world, sharing the simple truths of God's Word with people of various backgrounds. His "Gospel Truth" program is broadcasted on radio all across the nation, as well as on television in both the United States and Europe. "The Gospel Truth" can also be accessed on his website - www.awmi.net. He has distributed over three million cassette teaching tapes free of charge. In 1994, Andrew started Colorado Bible College, and has since then opened Charis Bible Colleges in England, Russia, and Portugal.

The Lord has given Andrew revelation knowledge and an anointing to present God's Word with simplicity and clarity. Wherever he travels, his powerful emphasis on the Word continues to set people free, often with signs and wonders following.